WACKY & WONDERFUL ROADSIDE ATTRACTIONS *of* ALASKA

 PHOTOGRAPHY AND STORIES BY HARRY M. WALKER

For Ringa . . . who is always ready to go.

Project Editor: Kent Sturgis
Text Editor: Kent Sturgis
Cover and Book Design: Elizabeth Watson
Proofreader: Sherrill Carlson
Printer: Samhwa Printing Co., Ltd., Seoul, Korea

Front cover: Santa's rocket ship at Mukluk Land; (clockwise from upper left), a bucket of flowers at the Crow Creek Mine; a totem in Klawock; Santa Claus statue in North Pole; a castle-like home in Homer.

PRINTED IN KOREA

First Printing, April 2002

10 9 8 7 6 5 4 3 2 1

To order single copies of WACKY & WONDERFUL ROADSIDE ATTRACTIONS OF ALASKA, mail $14.95 plus $4.95 for shipping (WA residents add $1.70 state sales tax) to: Epicenter Press, PO Box 82368, Kenmore, WA 98028.

Discover exciting ALASKA BOOK ADVENTURES! Visit our online Alaska bookstore and art gallery at www.EpicenterPress.com, or call our 24-hour, toll-free hotline at 800-950-6663

Booksellers: This title is available from major wholesalers. Retail discounts are available from our trade distributor, Graphic Arts Center Publishing Co., PO Box 10306, Portland, OR 97210. Phone 800-452-3032.

▶ A tongue-in-cheek sign (I hope) at a roadside business ▶ ▶ the road ahead at times seems endless.

FOREWORD

Flying over the Alaska terrain reveals a truth not entirely evident from the road: There is hardly anything here.

Rocks, trees, lakes, swamps, and tundra are etched at rare intervals by tiny veins of roadway with a few buildings dotted along them. Every once in awhile the dots form clusters, and those are towns. I've often said that civilization in Alaska is several thousand miles long and a hundred yards wide. Hang a random left or right turn at any intersection as you drive through Alaska and it won't be long before you're on your own.

Scrap metal doesn't fetch much of a price this far from the buyers, so big, heavy things no longer able to transport themselves tend to lie approximately where they died. Rusted cranes and exhausted Cadillacs sit side by side with more conventional visitor attractions. You often can buy bait, beer, ammo, and have your picture taken in front of a tractor tire filled with wild flowers all in one stop. Walt Disney never thought of that!

Unlike highways in the other 48 where roadside attractions can be a form of theater—the bold and the eccentric often drown out the more subdued local fare—Alaska's roadside attractions are more true to the place. They are the place. For better and for worse.

The best of it includes the most stunning views on the planet. The worst of it is always good for a few laughs. That's not a bad range to travel in.

—Tom Bodett, *Author and Radio Anomaly*

3

CONTENTS

12 Anyone with a strong constitution is welcome to drive over the collapsed Million Dollar Bridge.

18 Ethel looks good in an arctic fox bikini.

34 Dolly and Dolly's House in Ketchikan.

INTRODUCTION

For all its size (over 586,000 square miles) Alaska has less than 13,000 miles of road. By comparison, Texas, half the size of Alaska, has more than 293,000 miles of road. Still, Alaska has more than its share of roadside attractions. Admittedly there are no drive-through trees or mystery spots that defy the laws of nature, yet what other state can boast a four-story plywood igloo and a museum dedicated to ice?

As elsewhere, many roadside attractions in Alaska are roadside businesses, but not all businesses qualify as attractions. Roadside attractions in Alaska can be ordinary looking on the outside and sometimes downright ugly on the inside and yet there's something—usually the owner—that sets them apart.

In the 1920s and '30s while beer keg drive-ins, dinosaur gas stations, and sixty-five foot elephant motels were the

rage across America, log roadhouses were about all there was along Alaska's two roads—the Richardson and Steese highways—that totaled less than 600 miles. World War II brought new roads—the Alcan, Taylor, and Glenn highways—and new roadhouses but no roadside attractions. Road travel was still not for the faint of heart and simply getting somewhere in one piece was more important than eating in a drive-in in the shape of a hotdog.

The late 1970s and 1980s saw significant change along Alaska's roads. Construction of the trans-Alaska oil pipeline brought increased attention and more revenue to Alaska, which in turn brought increased traffic and better roads. At the same time a new crop of entrepreneurs—Vietnam vets hoping for a fresh start, pipeline construction workers flush with money, old-time Alaskans looking for something new—came along to open roadside businesses. Unfortunately creativity is no substitute for business skills, a good location and a bit of luck.

▲ Alaska's roadside attractions may not be much to look at but visitors are always welcome.
▶ There are "attractions" everywhere you look along the Denali Highway.

Many of these businesses went broke or were sold, though a few have endured to become some of Alaska's most popular roadside attractions.

By the mid-1990s big money, nearly all of it from outside of the state, discovered Alaska tourism and the look of Alaska's roadside businesses began to change once again. Idiosyncratic and original were being replaced with slick, packaged, and pretentious as big corporations tried to make Alaska's businesses look more like businesses everywhere else. Sad to say but perhaps Alaska's golden age of roadside attractions was over.

Move beyond the eclectic and sometimes eccentric and there are plenty of other potential roadside attractions. For example, in Alaska the old is rarely destroyed to make way for the new. The old is simply abandoned, much of it along Alaska's roads. From the end of the nineteenth century onward each successive boom—for gold, copper, fish and oil—has left reminders of great engineering feats, folly and greed. The combination makes for irresistible roadside attractions.

True also that fur-bikini-clad mannequins and abandoned railroad engines not withstanding no list of Alaska's roadside attractions would be complete without a few of Alaska's spectacular natural sites. Drive-up glaciers, rivers full of salmon and bears, canyons lined with waterfalls and North America's tallest peak qualify among Alaska's most compelling roadside attractions.

There are lots of other things that can be added to any list of roadside attractions in Alaska: roadside memorials, road signs, totem poles, churches, and mailboxes. The possibilities are endless. The truth is that like beauty, roadside attractions are in the eye of the beholder.

IGLOO CITY

George Parks Highway
near Cantwell

▲ ▲ A sign welcomes visitors to Igloo City.
▲ Leon Smith's dream igloo hotel never opened its doors for business.

Leon Smith had a dream to build the largest igloo in the world. It didn't matter that the igloo was mostly used in Greenland, not Alaska. According to Leon: "It's appropriate that Alaska have an igloo." 🚙 In the 1970s, Leon designed and started building his igloo along the George Parks Highway between Anchorage and Fairbanks. And not just any igloo, either. No, Leon's igloo would become a four-story hotel. He was certain lots of folks would stay a night or two just to be able to tell friends back home that they had stayed in an igloo during their visit to Alaska. 🚙 Leon's igloo was framed in wood and covered with 888 sheets of plywood. Then, the plywood was covered with urethane foam and painted white to give it a fresh snow look. The interior had a four-story atrium with forty-eight tiny pie-shaped rooms, with a dining room, kitchen, gift shop, and offices on the ground level. Leon's igloo had everything. Well almost everything. 🚙 When the building was inspected by the local fire marshal, Leon discovered that his igloo lacked something important—fire escapes. Leon could have covered the exterior with fire escapes but that would have ruined his vision of how an igloo hotel should look. So, the fire escapes were never added and the igloo just sits there, an unfulfilled dream. I suppose that's the way dreams are sometimes.

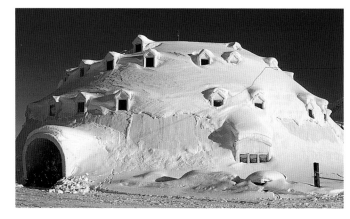

▲ Authorities told Leon his igloo needed fire escapes.

ROAD SIGNS

▲ (Clockwise) For those intrepid "hunters" for whom the smell of gunfire is an aphrodisiac, road signs are an irresistible attraction.

There are two "reasonable" explanations for the number of bullet-ridden signs found along Alaska's roads. Either there are a lot of frustrated hunters or quite a few armed passersby who have been forced to defend themselves against threatening road signs. Since a road sign has never attacked me I'm inclined to stick with the first explanation. 🚗 There appears to be an open season on road signs. Those for whom the smell of gunfire is an aphrodisiac find them to be an irresistible roadside attraction. Some of these intrepid "hunters" aren't satisfied until a road sign lies "dead" at their feet. Others are content to just wing a sign and leave it for someone else to finish off. 🚗 I think it's time to bring these people into the fold of legitimate hunting. Why not designate a hunting season on moose and caribou signs that coincides with the hunting season for the real thing? Why not make a few bucks for the state selling road-sign game tags? Right and left curve signs, the most abundant, would be the cheapest while pedestrian crossing signs, considering how rare they are, would be the most expen-

sive. Just think of all those brave marksmen out there waiting for the opportunity to entertain friends and family with stories of stalking a wily road-sign.

TRANS-ALASKA PIPELINE VIEWPOINT

Steese Highway, Fox

▲ ▲ Chelsea and Steve spend 10 hours a day answering questions.
▲ Pipeline "pigs" are inserted into the pipeline to clean out the inside of the pipe.

All the real action may take place hundreds of miles away at either end of the 800-mile trans-Alaska oil pipeline, but you wouldn't know it to watch the small parking lot at mile 8.4 of the Steese Highway north of Fairbanks. "I bet we must average about twenty-eight tour buses a day not counting stragglers who drive up on their own," Chelsea Bystedt, a visitor guide for Alyeska Pipeline Service Company, told me as we watched several buses unload their passengers. From mid-May until mid-September, Chelsea and fellow guide Steve Osborne spent 10 hours a day at the tiny visitor center answering thousands of questions. "Even though my parents met on the pipeline and both worked on the pipeline, I didn't know much about it until I started working here," Chelsea confided. Still, there are questions that no amount of study can prepare you for. For example, pipeline "pigs" are five-foot-long cylinders made of steel, rubber, and fiberglass that are inserted into the pipeline to clean out the inside of the pipe. People hear about pipeline pigs and think we send real pigs through the pipeline," Chelsea said, smiling. "I have to tell them we don't."

◀ Visitors inspect a section of the 800-mile pipeline that connects Prudhoe Bay with Valdez.

PEMRICH'S PETS

Farmers Loop,
Fairbanks

▲ One of the many stuffed animals saved by roadside "collector" Tom Pemrich.
▶ Tom nailed close to 300 stuffed animals to trees on his five-acre lot.

It may be hard to believe, given everything you hear or know about Alaska winters, but some Alaskans are a little bored by the predominance of green in summer. Tom Pemrich was. That's why he began nailing stuffed animals to the trees on his five-acre lot along Farmers Loop. Most roadside attractions are commercial in nature, but Tom Pemrich's collection of stuffed animals is on display there for no other purpose than to bring a smile and a little color to the lives of strangers. "I came up from Milwaukee in 1997 with one stuffed animal attached to my vehicle," Tom told me as we toured his roadside property. That was just the beginning. After numerous trips to Value Village, the Salvation Army, a bit of dumpster diving, and a few donations, Tom's collection had grown to about 284 stuffed animals — even Tom isn't exactly sure of the number. "There's Mickey Mouse, Taco Bell Dog, Wiley Coyote and Roger Rabbit," he said, pointing to a few of his favorites. "I just picked up Road Runner over there last week." Though tour buses drive by for a look, not everyone is happy with Tom's display. "The postman asked me to take down the twenty-seven stuffed animals I had on the mailbox," Tom said. "I know some people think the stuffed animals are an eyesore, but I make more people happy than I make mad." And what's wrong with that?

MILLION DOLLAR BRIDGE

Copper River Highway

near Cordova

▲ and ▶ Anyone with a strong constitution is welcome to drive over the collapsed bridge.

To complete a 193-mile railroad between the copper-rich Kennecott Mine near McCarthy and tidewater at Cordova, builders needed a bridge to cross the Copper River at a tight spot sandwiched between two active glaciers (Miles and Child's). People said the bridge couldn't be built. They were nearly right. Construction on the $1.5 million bridge began April 1, 1909 and proceeded through temperatures of 60 below, winds that exceeded 95 mph, and snows that accumulated to 34 feet. By mid-winter, Miles Glacier was advancing four feet per day, raising the water level of the river and pushing Copper River ice perilously close to the bridge. Thirty men with steam points and chisels worked in 24-hour shifts to relieve pressure on the construction pilings and falsework that held together the partially built bridge. The last bolt on the bridgework was driven into place one hour before breakup. Despite the extraordinary effort made to build it, the railroad operated only twenty-eight years until the copper mine closed in 1938. Lest anyone doubt the permanence of the closure, the rails were pulled up shortly after the outbreak of World War II, loaded onto a barge, and promptly lost in a storm in the Gulf of Alaska. After the war, construction began on a road that followed the old railroad

right-of-way all the way to Chitina. By 1958, the first 48 miles from Cordova to the bridge were completed. But the project was shaken when one of the bridge spans collapsed into the Copper River during the powerful Good Friday Earthquake in 1964. Shortly afterward a temporary roadway was put in place to enable anyone with a strong constitution to drive across the collapsed span. And while talk continues about repairing the bridge properly and finishing the road to Chitina, that temporary patch has become, at least for now, a permanent fixture.

▼ The dream of seeing a road between Cordova and Chitna was shaken by the Good Friday Earthquake in 1964.

KNOTTY SHOP

Richardson Highway
at Salcha

▲ and ▶ Spruce burls and ice cream are the "thing" at the Knotty Shop.

Fairbanks taxidermist Jim Rothenbuhler had outgrown his shop. Wife Paula wanted a way out of teaching. So in 1978 Jim and Paula looked south 32 miles to Salcha, a small community strung out along Richardson Highway near the Salcha River. For Jim there was plenty of room for a bigger shop and for Paula space for a little gift shop stocked with strictly Alaska-made items. 🚙 Paula and Jim soon realized that to draw local folks from Fairbanks or travelers off the highway in the middle of nowhere they would need "something," maybe more than one "something." With a bit of inspiration Paula and Jim came up with an unconventional combination of "something's" that has kept them jumping at the Knotty Shop for years. 🚙 "Spruce burl animals and ice cream," Paula told me with a big smile. 🚙 "I didn't know about Jim's thing with burls when we got married," Paula admitted. "He's always loved wood and woodworking. He made little stuff with burls—clocks and coffee tables. Then he used them in the construction of the building . . .

and the animals sort of just happened." 🚙 "The moose, caribou, and sheep were easy to do," Paula said, "the horns help to identify them. After the sheep he did a mos-

quito—the wings helped that one. The other one with the wings is a no-see-um. He tried to do a bear, but it looks like a pig. The wolf—well, nobody knows what that one is." 🚙 The ice cream just happened too. "Jim found this great burl," Paula said, "and when he slabbed it he thought it would make a great counter. But then when we put the 30-foot thing in, we thought: 'What are we going to do with it?' That's when we got the idea to sell ice cream. We give a big scoop for a dollar and people drive out from town just for the ice cream. We can do a thousand scoops in a day. 🚙 Originally I thought I would put a love seat and small table just inside the front door of the

place so that I could sit and embroider until the occasional customer came in," Paula said wistfully. "Boy, that never worked out."

◀ ◀ Jim thought the big burl would make a great counter. But what to do with it?

◀ Jim and Paula Rothenbuhler built and operate the Knotty Shop.

WAL-MIKE'S

George Parks Highway
at Trapper Creek

▲ A tongue-in-cheek sign (?) at Wal-Mikes.

▶ At 5:00 P.M. on October 15, 1997, Mike's contract postal station became Wal-Mike's.

When Mike Carpenter first came north from Anchorage in 1965 to the portion of an old homestead he occupies at the corner of the George Parks Highway and the Petersville Road, there was no George Parks Highway or Petersville Road. Not yet anyway. "There was a lot of romance up here before the highway—no road, no electric, no phone," said Mike. 🚙 That changed in 1971, and Mike and the Parks Highway have struggled to come to terms with each other ever since. It hasn't always been easy. "I've said this a million times a poor boy has the right to make a living along the side of the road. You have

the right to go broke in this country," Mike told me. 🚙 With the coming of the highway came a spurt of growth to Trapper Creek. Mike went into hardware and lumber for a while, then in 1978 built a 12- by 16-foot building and became a contractor for the U.S. Postal Service. "I was selling stuff and doing the post office at the same time." That lasted nearly 20 years. 🚙 In 1997, he lost the contract. "October 15, 1997—that was the day I stopped doing the post office at 4:00 P.M. and by 5:00 P.M. I was Wal-Mike's." 🚙 "All the stuff in here is on consignment," Mike continued. "All the nice stuff is mine. All the junk belongs to my neighbors, and they love bringing it. I'd like to open upstairs when I get crowded out down here." 🚙 It's hard to imagine that day can be far off. During the hour or so I spent with Mike, one guy stopped by for a cooler, another wanted a fitting for a propane stove, still another dropped off a pile of old downhill skis, and someone offered some honey for sale. "I get days when I run ragged." 🚙 There are times when Mike wonders if the struggle to keep going on his spot at the crossroads is worth the effort. "Many times I'll get a little discouraged but then I'll have a talk with myself and things will be okay."

◀ "I'd like to open upstairs when I get crowded out down here," Mike said.

▲ "All the stuff here is on consignment. All the nice stuff is mine. All the junk belongs to my neighbors."

FUR SHACK

Richardson Highway
just north of Delta
Junction.

▲ "Ethel" looks good in an arctic
fox bikini.
▶ Kathy makes nearly all the
items for sale at the Fur Shack.
▶ ▶ Kathy and Steve have little
trouble getting people to stop with
Ethel out front to catch their eye.

Despite the negativity about furs in most other places, trapping is a proud and continuing tradition in Alaska. "We named it the Fur Shack so people know what's here—no surprises," Kathy Fields told me, referring to the . . . well, the shack she and husband Steve operate as a store next to the Richardson Highway. Kathy and Steve bought the Fur Shack in 1992. "We started in the brown shack next door," Kathy said, pointing to a still smaller building next to hers. "I was doing crochet then. Now I make all of the fur and leather products and the porcelain dolls. We get the furs from trappers in the Fairbanks area

already tanned." 🚙 People's trepidation about furs aside, Kathy and Steve have little trouble getting people to stop, not with Ethel out front to catch the eye of passing motorists. 🚙 Ethel, a fur-bikini-wearing mannequin named for a character in a 1970s Ray Stevens song, is a permanent fixture at the Fur Shack, though Kathy says wind, dust, rain, and sun take their toll. "She's been completely refurbished at least a couple of times. We replace her bathing suit every year." 🚙 Do people ever ask to buy a fur bikini? You bet. "We have just two left right now," Kathy said. "The arctic fox she's wearing goes for $250." In case you're wondering.

SHEEP VIEWING

Seward Highway
along Turnagain Arm

▲ and ▶ Dall sheep and human climbers frequent the mountainsides along Turnagain Arm.

As a teenager in New York City, I would go with friends into Manhattan where we would stand on a corner, stare intently up at a building, and point without saying a word. Before long, strangers eager to be a part of the action were looking up and pointing as well, though they had no idea what they were looking at. After a few minutes we would slip away and watch as the "event" took on a life of its own. In New York, the prank never failed. I mention this because while driving along Turnagain Arm on the Seward Highway the thought of those innocent bystanders being suckered into my teenage prank comes to mind. 🚙 Dall Sheep, critters known for living on steep rocks, frequent the mountainsides along Turnagain Arm. Summer or winter you can drive the highway just south of Anchorage and see folks pulled over pointing up to a spot on the cliffs. Moms with lambs, more tolerant of humans than the big rams, come remarkably close to the road. In winter, when heavy snow up high forces them down from their usual haunts, even the big boys will make an appearance. 🚙 Still, there are times driving along the highway that it is difficult to see what everyone is pointing at. Luckily, I overcome my New York skepticism and pull over to get a view of a wonderful roadside attraction.

DENALI VIEWPOINT

Mile 135 George
Parks Highway

▶ Denali Viewpoint is the place to see the mountain—when you can.

Alaskans know the mountain as Denali from an Indian word meaning "The High One." Officially, however, it is Mount McKinley, renamed in 1896 for a U.S. president who never stepped foot in Alaska. 🚙 Nearly four miles high, Denali dominantes the landscape for thousands of square miles. Without doubt, it is Alaska's premier roadside attraction. And though visible from Anchorage, Fairbanks, and many highway points in between, Denali Viewpoint, a large paved turnout at milepost 135 of the George Parks Highway, is certainly the busiest and likely the best spot along Alaska's road system to view the 20,320-foot peak. 🚙 Often obscured by clouds of its own making, the mountain is out of sight two of three days in summer, and the odds are only slightly better of seeing it in winter. 🚙 Still, on any given summer day, hundreds, perhaps thousands, of folks pull off the highway at Denali Viewpoint. Some bring home a photo of the mountain like a trophy. Most others simply gaze in the mountain's general direction and wonder where it went.

I.R.B.I.

Mile 20 Seward Highway
near Moose Pass

▲ Irvin built the 27-foot wooden knife to attract attention.
▶ Irvin and Virgil have transformed auto springs, chainsaw bars and big timing chains into more than 18,000 knives.

For more than thirty years, Irvin Campbell and more recently his son Virgil have transformed worn automobile springs, chainsaw bars, and even timing chains from the engines of state ferries into beautiful knives of all shapes and sizes. 🚙 Irvin, who wanted to be a lion tamer until his wife put her foot down, taught himself to make knives by reading books. After much trial and error, Irvin was confident enough to give his knives a lifetime guarantee—for the lifetime of the maker, that is, as the elder Campbell used to say. Now that a second generation of Campbells is making knives, Virgil says that warranty has been extended. 🚙 Having made more than 18,000 knives between them, the Campbells have their business well established and Virgil admits that these days his knives pretty much sell themselves. But that wasn't always the case. 🚙 In the 1970s, Irvin decided he needed something to attract attention. "Dad built the twenty-seven-foot wooden knife," Virgil said, referring to the sign at the edge

of the Seward Highway. "At first, he told the neighbors he was building an airplane and that was the wing." 🚙 And what about the name I.R.B.I.? According to Virgil, that was a last minute thing. "Irvin and his brother Bill were going to go into the knife business together," Virgil said. "Bill backed out at the last minute and left Dad with a bunch of signs with their names on it. Dad just wouldn't let them go to waste." And so with a little imagination and a bit of paint Virgil and Bill became I.R. and B.I.

HOOK, LINE, AND SINKER

Valdez

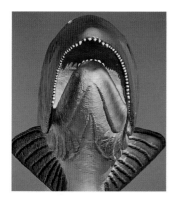

▲ and ▶ The 28-foot fiberglass pink salmon has been known to fool some visitors, some of the time.

"We are the pink salmon capital of the world," David Winney, store manager of a fishing supply store known as the Hook, Line, and Sinker, told me as we spoke at his front counter. "We average about 10 to 12 million pinks a year because of the hatchery (at Solomon Gulch)." 🚙 That goes a long way to explain the twenty-eight-foot-long pink salmon just outside the building made of fiberglass, re-bar, and plywood. "We had the thing done seventeen years ago by Arctic Fox Taxidermy up in Wasilla," David said. " It does help get people in the store." 🚙 Of course, you expect a giant fish sitting fifteen feet off the ground to draw more than fishermen looking to purchase a few fishing doodads. "Lots of people get their picture taken holding their hands up over their heads as if they were holding up the fish," David explained. 🚙 And though pink salmon weigh four to eight pounds on average, there's always somebody who believes the fish is real. "Carloads of people come by and there's always one person. . . . " David said with a smile. "Usually the rest of the group will set him straight. But once in a while we get someone who's by himself and we kid him along." 🚙 I guess you can say that they get the guy to swallow the story hook, line, and sinker.

MENDENHALL GLACIER

Mendenhall Loop
Road near Juneau

▲ Mendenhall Glacier has retreated 2 1/2 miles since 1750.
▶ Each year 300,000 people visit this river of ice.

Seattle has its drive-up espresso stands, Las Vegas drive-up wedding chapels, and California . . . well, California may have a drive-up for just about anything, but none have Alaska's drive-up glaciers. 🚙 Mendenhall Glacier is one of more than thirty glaciers that squeeze like toothpaste from the 1,500-square-mile Juneau Ice Field, an area larger than Rhode Island. Just twelve miles from downtown Juneau, Mendenhall is one of Alaska's most approachable glaciers. 🚙 Each year, 300,000 people visit this river of ice by bus or car and hundreds more on foot, bikes, roller skates, and cross-country skis in winter.

Yet, with each passing year, Mendenhall becomes less approachable. Until 1750, the glacier was advancing, its face nearly two and half miles closer to where Juneau was to be settled in the nineteenth century. Since then, the glacier has retreated steadily—nearly three hundred feet in 2000 alone. In all the face has pulled back nearly a half mile from where it was when the visitor center was built in 1962. At some point in the not so distant future, the visitor center may have to be moved just to keep the glacier in view. Perhaps then they could include a drive-up wedding chapel and espresso stand. Wouldn't that be something?

▼ Mendenhall Glacier is one of more than 30 glaciers that flow from the Juneau Ice field.

CHILKAT BALD EAGLE PRESERVE

Haines Highway north
of Haines

▲ and ▶ As many as 4,000 eagles gather at the eagle preserve each winter.

Travel north on the Haines Highway about twenty miles from the town of Haines between mid-October and the end of December and you are guaranteed to see bald eagles. Lots and lots of bald eagles. Because warm springs keep the Chilkat River from freezing, chum salmon spawn there later in the year than they do anywhere within a thousand miles. For an eagle looking to make it through a long winter, that's an irresistible dinner invitation. In recent years, as many as 4,000 eagles have gathered on the preserve, mostly within a 4,800-acre area known as the Bald Eagle Council Grounds. Natives from the nearby village of Klukwan say that in the good old days (before the White Man arrived), 4,000 eagles would have been an

insignificant number. You might assume thousands of eagles feeding on salmon would create a spectacle. In truth, the eagles spend a lot of time doing, well . . . nothing. To do otherwise would cause the eagles to expend energy they would rather not expend in winter. So, even though there are tons of live spawning salmon available, the eagles prefer spawned-out chum salmon carcasses along the riverbank. That might seem a bit strange, but why work for a meal when you can waddle up to the buffet table?

PATSY ANN

Cruise Ship Dock,
Juneau

▲ and ▶ More than 50 years after her death Patsy Ann continues to greet all visitors to the Juneau waterfront.

From about 1932 until her death a decade later, an English Bull Terrier named Patsy Ann faithfully greeted every ship to arrive at the docks in downtown Juneau. Though she had no owner, Patsy Ann appeared to have the run of homes and businesses all over town and for much of her life she chose to live at the Longshoremen's Hall. She was a favorite subject of photographers, shops sold postcards of her, and the local newspaper wrote about her adventures. Patsy Ann was so faithful to her adopted purpose that in 1934 the mayor dubbed her "Official Greeter of Juneau," and when a city ordinance required a license for every canine in town, Patsy Ann got a special exemption. As amazing as this story may be, there is one more detail that makes the Patsy Ann story even more amazing. Patsy Ann was profoundly deaf from birth, yet she seemed to "hear" the whistles of approaching boats a half-mile away. It's said that one time when a crowd gathered at the wrong dock to await an approaching ship, Patsy Ann—after hesitating for a moment—proceeded to the correct one. On the fiftieth anniversary of her death, a nearly five-foot bronze statue of Patsy Ann was erected on the cruise ship dock. Once again, passersby can give her a little pat or a hug, and sit beside her for a photo. And while it's true that she still can't hear a thing, it's also true that she never misses an arrival.

SANTA CLAUS HOUSE

Richardson Highway
at North Pole

In the late 1940s, a handful of folks with more ambition than reason decided that naming their tiny town North Pole would lure toy manufacturers. Of course, to toy-makers based in New York and Chicago, relocating to North Pole, Alaska made about as much sense as relocating to the real North Pole. 🚙 Then fate took a hand. In 1952, as fancy new stores made his Fairbanks trading post obsolete, Con Miller moved his family fourteen miles south to North Pole in hope of starting over. As the story is told, for years Con had been playing Santa Claus for kids in Interior Alaska villages as he made his way around trading for furs. One day, as he and his sons were building their new building in North Pole, a truckload of Native kids drove by, and somebody called out, "Hello Santa Claus! Are you building a new house?" And right then and there the idea to combine Santa, a gift shop, and the town of North Pole was conceived. 🚙 As word of Santa Claus House in North Pole spread, the business grew into the biggest gift shop in Interior Alaska. In 1971, a new four-lane highway bypassed the town and the original log building. Once again, Con moved the family, this time to a bigger and better location facing the Richardson Highway. 🚙 According to daughter Merry (yes, Con named her Merry

▲ Santa Claus House has been located along the Richardson Highway since 1971.

28

Christmas Miller in 1961), Con "was always coming up with new ideas." One of his ideas in the early 1950s was letters from Santa that could be postmarked "North Pole, Alaska". 🚙 "Originally, the letters were hand-written," Merry told me. "Everyone in the family wrote letters starting in October." By the early 1990s, the volume had reached 40,000 letters a year, and Santa was forced to go high tech with a computer.

🚙 Though Con Miller died in 1996 at age eighty-five, Santa Claus House remains a family business. "When I was maybe six or seven," said Merry, "I got a red velvet suit and got to sit next to Santa and give out candy canes." She's been hooked ever since.

◄ ◄ The gift shop grew into the biggest in Interior Alaska.
◄ It's always Christmas at Santa Claus House.
▶ Passersby can't miss the big fiberglass Santa along the side of the road.

TOTEM PARK

Klawock on Prince of
Wales Island

▲ Twenty-one poles have been
erected in the totem park.

The totem park in Klawock is an archive full of stories. One totem pole there tells of a brave young man who catches a lake monster in a trap. Another relates how raven turns himself into a woman to marry a brown bear. A third how Natsihlane makes the first killer whale. These are stories full of bravery and stupidity, death and creation, happiness and sorrow. 🚙 Not having a written language, the Tlingit people of Prince of Wales Island carved totem poles to preserve family records, clan histories, and cultural myths. Prior to contact with outsiders, a lack of suitable tools, wealth, and leisure time kept carving projects to a minimum. After contact, things changed and by the end of the nineteenth century the size and beauty of totem poles became displays of wealth and status. 🚙 Historically, Tlingits migrated seasonally between Klawock and Tuxekan, farther north on the island. When the people decided to live in Klawock year-round, the totem poles were left behind at Tuxekan. But leaving the poles behind was like abandoning a library, so the people later moved them, many in poor condition, to a spot overlooking Klawock Inlet. Twenty-one totem poles have been erected in the park, and many have been painstaking restored or duplicated. 🚙 Like a foreign-language film with no subtitles, the meaning of many of the totems is

◀ Totem poles tell stories full of bravery and stupidity, death and creation, happiness and sorrow.

sadly lost on most visitors. Still, there are plenty of eagles, ravens, bears, dogs, and mythical animals to identify and to wonder about. Have you ever heard the story about the Tlingit maiden and the woodworm?

HYDER BEARS

Fish Creek at Mile 6

Salmon Glacier Road

▶ At any time a hundred people mill around behind the bushes along the road waiting to see a bear.

Bear viewing at Fish Creek near Hyder is like standing outside the Kodak Theater on Oscar night—lots of waiting around followed by jostling to get a glimpse of a star strolling by on the red carpet. At Fish Creek, the celebrities are brown and black bears looking for a meal of fresh salmon and the creek, well . . . that's as close to a red carpet as you will find in Hyder. "People have been watching bears at Fish Creek for years," Paul Larkin, head of the Hyder office of the U.S. Forest Service told me. "In the old days, locals would go up to the creek, set up a barbecue, and watch bears." 🚙 Today however, with thousands of visitors a year there's no room for such casualness. The tiny parking lot next to the road fills early. By mid-afternoon, a line of cars, trucks, and motor homes

stretches down Salmon Glacier Road. At any time, a hundred people mill around behind the bushes along the road waiting for a bear to break out of the trees on the far side of the creek. 🚙 Cruising along in the shallow water looking for salmon, the bears seem oblivious to the entourage of humans on the road twenty feet away cruising right along with them. Most of the time, the bears stay on the creek and the people stay on the road, but not always. According to Paul, a young bear occasionally will come up to the road and mingle with his fans. Forest Service rangers do their best to keep the two species apart. 🚙 Amazingly, there's never been a serious problem with a bear, which says far more about the remarkable tolerance of bears than it does about the common sense of humans.

◀ and ▲ Bears fishing for salmon are the star attractions at Fish Creek.

DOLLY'S HOUSE

Creek Street in
Ketchikan

▲ The services available at
Dolly's House have changed
over the years but the price is
pretty close to the same.
▶ "It's hard work being a
floozy," says Linda Elliot.

The red light district on Creek Street was one of Ketchikan's biggest attractions during the first half of the twentieth century, especially among the men of Alaska's fishing fleet. More than thirty houses of ill repute lined both sides of the creek. Closest to the waterfront was Dolly's House, built in 1906 and purchased by Dolly Arthur in 1919. Dolly, who operated No. 24 Creek Street on her own until the district was closed down in 1954, was one of the most popular and therefore one of the busiest women on the street, entertaining from fifteen to twenty men a night. Dolly is quoted as having said: "I liked it here because the

If you can't find your husband... He's in here!

men came in bunches." In addition to being a successful businesswoman, Dolly was a bit of a visionary as well. Her will specified that her house on Creek Street couldn't be sold from the estate unless the buyer promised to keep it and all of its furnishings forever a residence/museum. Though other houses on Creek Street have been torn down or converted to gift shops, only Dolly's House remains untouched. The spirit if not the profession lives on through Linda Elliott, madam curator of the Dolly House Museum. Linda spends her days standing in the doorway of No. 24 posing for photos, and enticing people to spend $4 (in 1919, Dolly charged $3 for her services) for a self-guided tour through a bit of Alaska history. "What a great job," Linda told me. "I wear feathers, smoke cigarettes, and talk dirty all day." On busy summer days she performs non-stop for hours. "It's hard work being a floozy, but I love what I do."

▼ No. 24 was one of the busiest houses of ill-repute in Ketchikan's red-light district.

BIRD CREEK

Seward Highway

▲ John holds a silver salmon he just pulled from Bird Creek.
▶ Five-year old Amelia wanted to fish just like the rest of her family.

For many Alaskans, only two summer-time activities are worth mentioning—going fishing or talking about going fishing. So it's no surprise that any river, creek, or stream that's home to more than a single fish has the potential to draw a crowd. Bird Creek, just 25 miles south of Anchorage on the Seward Highway, is one of Alaska's biggest roadside fishing attractions. During the annual salmon run hundreds of fishermen line the creek and, at low tide, the mud flats where the creek enters Turnagain Arm. 🚙 Gretchen and John Hennessy and their four children—Andrew, Larisa, Becca, and little five-year-old Amelia—had just moved to Anchorage from Boston and lost no time "going native." One of their first stops was Bird Creek. "I never figured we would catch anything," Gretchen told me as we watched her husband pull a silver salmon out of the creek to go with Andrew's pink. Gretchen scrunched her face. "I hope we don't catch too many. I don't know what we'll do with them." 🚙 "Amelia hasn't had as much experience fishing as her siblings but she's game," John told me. "We tried to get her to come today without a rod, but she wouldn't have it. She wanted to fish just like her brother and sisters." 🚙 As the rising tide flooded the mud flats and

the lower banks of the creek, fishermen scrambled upstream. Amelia seemed oblivious to the goings on around her, casting a foot or two away, reeling in her line after a couple of seconds only to repeat the process again. 🚙 "The little one is fishing without a hook but she doesn't know it," John said, his voice brimming with a father's love.

▼ During the annual salmon run hundreds of fishermen line the creek.

GLACIER PARK RESORT

Just off the Glenn Highway

▶ Lots of folks pay to use the road that leads up to the face of Matanuska Glacier.

"How much to get to the glacier?" the guy in motorcycle leathers asked. 🚙 "It's $8 for one adult and $6 for a child or a senior if you've got one tucked away somewhere I can't see," Shelly Shorten answered, standing behind the counter in the office of the Glacier Park Resort. 🚙 "Thanks," he said, walking back to his motorcycle. 🚙 "He was pretty nice," Shelly said to me. "Usually they're pretty rude. They don't think anyone should own a glacier. They don't bother to find out that we don't own the glacier, just the road up to it." 🚙 The glacier in question is the Matanuska Glacier, a 24 mile-long river of ice that flows out of the Chugach Mountains in the Chugach National Forest, some 100 miles

northeast of Anchorage along the Glenn Highway. The road in question, all two miles of it, was built and is still owned by Jack Kimball, who homesteaded six hundred acres strategically located between two channels of the Matanuska River smack dab in front of the glacier. Shelly's sister, Kelly, and husband Bill Stevenson have leased the resort (which is little more than the road) for the past six years.  "We get between 100 to 150 people through here a day at the peak of the season," Shelly told me. That makes the Glacier Park Resort road one of the most valuable private roads in Alaska. A guy from Palmer I met in the parking lot at the end of the road had just returned from a hike on the glacier with six members of his family. "I don't think you should have to pay to get to a glacier," he said. "Then again if this is private property then the owner should have something to say about who crosses it. Truth is, I wish I owned it."

▲ Shelly Shorten and friend at the Glacier Park Resort office.

CROW CREEK MINE

Crow Creek Road

near Girdwood

▲ Patty looks for a little "color" in the bottom of a gold pan.
▶ ▲ Signs explain the "bill of faire" at the Crow Creek Mine.
▶ This mine has a lush garden.

Although the Crow Creek Mine is located some four miles from Girdwood on a poorly maintained gravel road, more than 20,000 people a year visit this old gold mine to soak up a little gold rush ambiance. Since the late 1890s, the mine has been worked by hundreds of miners who stayed a while and then moved on, leaving everything behind. Old stuff is literally everywhere. The Toohey family, which has operated the sixty-acre mine site as a tourist attraction since 1969, has worked hard to share with visitors the history and culture of gold mining along Crow Creek. As Cynthia Toohey, matriarch of the family, was once

quoted as saying: "We mine tourists here now, not gold." That's not to say that there isn't gold along Crow Creek. There is, and nearly everyone who visits tests his skill with a gold pan. Most are satisfied with a plastic bag of dirt guaranteed to have a few flakes, a gold pan, and a visit to the panning shed (a large wooden sink with running water). The more serious visitors are encouraged to grab a shovel, gold pan, and perhaps a miniature sluice (a device to separate out the gold bearing gravel) and make their way down to Crow Creek for a couple of hours of earnest effort. "It's fun," said Chuck Haddox, an ex-Alaskan from Denver, visiting with his wife Eleanor, daughter Patty, and grandsons Tyler and Casey, all of whom spent a pleasant sunny afternoon working the creek. "You just have to be patient to make anything." "We brought the kids, but I think Grandma and Grandpa are having more fun," said Eleanor, as the two boys took a nap under a pile of towels and jackets. "The kids lasted a couple of hours," said Patty. "They found a little gold in the plastic bags of dirt. That made them happy." What will the family do with its hard-earned riches? "We'll probably give the gold to the kids so that they can bring it to school for shown-and-tell," said Eleanor.

▶ Patty, Eleanor and Chuck wash Crow Creek looking for gold.

SHRINE OF SAINT THERESE

Glacier Highway north
of Juneau

▲ The chapel was to be built from logs until D.P. "Doc" Holden decided to use beach stone.
▶ and ▶ ▶ After the roof and walls were completed, the solid rock floor was blasted to make way for a crypt.
▶ ▶ ▶ After years of effort Crow Island was connected to the mainland by a causeway.

Since 1941, the Shrine of Saint Therese has offered the people of Juneau a special place of serenity and contemplation. Named for a Carmelite nun from Lisieux, France who died in 1897 at the age of twenty-four, the shrine was dedicated to her rather unusual message that God especially loves "ordinary" people because He created so many of them. 🚗 The site selected in 1932 was tiny Crow Island, some 23 miles north of Juneau After years of effort, the island was connected to the mainland by a causeway, and work began on the shrine in 1937. 🚗 Like nearly all buildings of the time in Alaska, the chapel was to be

built of logs—that is, until D.P. "Doc" Holden, a skilled stone mason, volunteered to be foreman of the project, and the use of logs was dropped in favor of beach stone. Limited to volunteer labor and little equipment, work on the walls dragged on for more than two years. 🚙 Once the walls and roof were completed a last-minute decision was made to add crypts under the shrine. Since the chapel was built on solid rock, the only way to accomplish this was to blow a hole in the floor from the inside, not exactly a routine procedure. With more than a little luck and a good deal of skill the chief blaster from the nearby A-J gold mine so carefully crafted the blast that the only damage to the entire building was a single chip knocked out of one of the roof trusses by flying rock. 🚙 Oh, the amazing things that "ordinary" people can accomplish.

MUKLUK LAND

Alaska Highway,
near Tok

▲ George whips up some cotton candy for a visitor.
▶ "Mukluk Land is a combination museum and amusement park," George said.

Asked to describe the park he and wife Beth created in 1985, George Jacobs told me: "Mukluk Land is a combination museum and amusement park, with a little humor and education thrown in." That pretty much says it. 🚙 George and Beth built Mukluk Land to fill what they perceived as a need. "I watched tourists coming through town with nothing to do," said George. 🚙 "Our main objective was for people to have a good time," Beth added. 🚙 The first piece they got for the four-acre park was an old truck. "Someone was going to bury it," George said. "I hauled it here." 🚙 The collection grew. Want to see the building used for Tok's first gift shop? They have it, as well as the building that housed Tok's first jail. In one corner of the park called Heater Heaven is a display of old wood stoves, boilers, and propane heaters. In another is a display of about

3,000 dolls that the couple bought from a woman who had salvaged them, perhaps individually, from a dump. Everywhere you look are old snow machines, old boats, old everything. And then there's the forty-foot "Santa's rocket ship" they found in a Wisconsin farm field. Over time, Beth and George added a large inflated igloo that the local kids use like an enclosed trampoline, a miniature golf course, and coin-fed Ski Ball games in the front office. More Alaskana shows up at Mukluk Land all the time. "At first I went around looking for stuff," said George, "but now most people who have something to put in the dump come here first. If I keep getting more stuff we'll expand." "He is still visualizing new things," Beth confided with a smile. "His brain never stops."

◄ ▲ Beth works the front office at Mukluk Land.
◄ ◄ Part of a collection of 3,000 dolls that were salvaged from a dump.
◄ Santa's rocket ship is a key attraction at Mukluk Land.

ICE ART MUSEUM

Fairbanks

▶ Richard encourages visitors to walk through the exhibits to get a feel for Fairbanks in winter.

One evening Richard Brickley, chairman of Ice Alaska, the organization that sponsors the annual World Ice Art Championship, was having dinner in a local restaurant with his wife, Hao. "We overheard a bus load of people talking about how wonderful it is here in the summer and wondering what it is like in winter." Right then and there, Richard got the idea for the Ice Art Museum. 🚗 You might expect, as I did, that an ice art museum open in the summer would be filled with photographs of ice art, perhaps a few ice-carving

tools, and not much else. For Richard, that simply wouldn't do. 🚙 In 1993, Richard bought the old Lacey Street Theater, originally opened in 1939 and closed since 1976, to house his new museum. He had two big glass-fronted cold rooms built. One was designed to replicate the average daytime temperatures in Fairbanks around the time of the ice-carving competition in March (18 to 20 degrees Fahrenheit), the other to replicate average nighttime temperatures (0 to -5 degrees). Each February since 1995, he has bought fifteen 4- by 4- by 3-foot blocks of ice, each weighing 3,700 pounds, stored them underneath insulating sawdust until June, when they are delivered to the museum. Then Richard hires local ice sculptors to come and do their thing. 🚙 Richard encourages visitors, most in shirt sleeves and some wearing shorts, to walk through the exhibits to get a feel (however briefly) for Fairbanks in March. The opportunity comes with just one piece of valuable advice: "Don't stick your tongue on the ice."

◄ and ► Every summer local ice sculptors come into the museum to do their work.

DENALI HIGHWAY

▲ There was a time when this highway was an important road but no more.
▶ A trip along the Denali Highway is an experience one should savor.

Back in the 1950s and '60s, the Denali Highway was one of the most important roads in Alaska—the only road link to Denali National Park. Folks headed for the remote park from Anchorage had two options. They could load their vehicle onto an Alaska Railroad flat car, traveling north by rail about 235 miles to the park entrance. Or, they could drive—189 miles east to Glennallen, 71 miles north on the Richardson Highway to Paxson, and finally 160 miles back west on the Denali Highway. A drive to the park from Fairbanks was only slightly less roundabout. 🚙 The George Parks Highway was built in

the late 1960s to provide a direct connection between Anchorage and Fairbanks by road. Once opened in 1971, its direct access to the park figuratively and literally cut the Denali Highway out of the loop. Since then, the lonely road has been largely forgotten (at least where state highway spending is concerned), though it is one of the most beautiful drives in the world. 🚙 With few people living along the gravel highway (a term used rather loosely in Alaska) the Denali remains a seasonal road. For years there has been talk about paving it. But there isn't much incentive to pave or keep open in the winter a road where few people live and there isn't much incentive to live along a road that's closed seven months a year. More recently there has even been talk about eliminating the funds needed to clear the road of snow each spring. That would effectively delay the road's opening from mid-May until mid-June, making an already short season even shorter. 🚙 Even when the Denali Highway is open, road conditions are, to put it kindly . . . rough. Though the posted speed limit is 50 miles per hour only a few daredevils are brave enough (or foolish enough) to go that fast. And that may be a good thing. 🚙 A trip on the Denali Highway is an experience one should savor like dinner in a fine restaurant — slowly.

DOWNTOWN CHICKEN

Taylor Highway

▲ The name "Downtown Chicken" was meant to be a joke.
▶ and ▶ ▲ At any time, more than one hundred hungry and thirsty people may drop in.

"I came from running a bookstore in Princeton, New Jersey to living a subsistence life on the Forty-Mile River," Susan Wren told me. "The change was just too extreme for me. My husband was never around, and I needed to talk to people." Chicken, a nearby community with a seasonal road, seemed the answer. 🚙 So, in 1988, Susan (and her husband) bought the only bar and restaurant in Chicken. In fact, except for a post office and a one-room school, it was the only anything in Chicken. "We made up the name 'Downtown Chicken'," Susan said. "It was meant to be a joke." 🚙 Susan soon discovered that running the only bar and restaurant for at least 100 miles in any direction in gold-mining country presented challenges which, like most things in her life, she met head on. 🚙 First, she made the bar more welcoming to visitors. "When I

first bought the bar," she admitted, "I was afraid to walk into the place. I cleaned out the rowdies."  Second, she addressed her serious lack of experience in the kitchen. "I taught myself how to bake and to make soup and stuff." The specialty of the house? Chicken soup, of course. Susan admits that the key to her success was persuading Princess Tours to stop on their way to and from Eagle on the Yukon River. At any one time, a couple of buses carrying more than one hundred hungry and thirsty people might appear at her door. It took some talking to convince Princess executives that she could handle that many folks at once. It wasn't long however before people on the buses were saying that Downtown Chicken had the most efficient operation they had seen on their travels. "I've learned that time is the most important thing to the buses." Despite doing everything right and maybe because of it, a new challenge had arisen when I visited. Two competing businesses had opened nearby, both also claiming to be in the real downtown Chicken. "I don't mind competition," Susan said. "I like it." You can almost believe she does.

◀ ▲ and ▲ Chickens are an important theme in Downtown Chicken.
◀ The first thing Susan did when she bought the bar was clean out the rowdies.

HOT SPOT CAFÉ

Mile 60 Dalton Highway

▶ The Hot Spot Café is an odd collection of buildings left over from pipeline construction days.

The Hot Spot Café may serve the best hamburgers in Alaska, and no one is more surprised about it than owner Theresa Morin. "I failed home-ec," she told me as she hustled around her odd collection of buildings just off the highway that connects the oil fields at Prudhoe Bay with Fairbanks. "My mother can't believe I'm doing this." "This" was born out of Theresa's wish to spend summers closer to her husband, a DOT (Department of Transportation) employee who works a couple of miles up the highway. With good food, heck . . . any food, as scarce as hen's teeth on the highway, a restaurant seemed like a good idea. Even a restaurant made from a surplus electric Incinolet incinerating toilet building left over from pipeline construction days. From the start, truckers making runs to Prudhoe Bay have been Theresa's biggest supporters. "Big-State Logistics shipped it (the restaurant) up on a semi, no charge, just to get us started in 1995," she said. "Every year since we've added a

building or two—a place to eat out of the rain, a gift shop, and motel rooms." The buildings, all pipeline surplus, were given to Theresa and trucked to the site for free. The only fly in the ointment is that Theresa has been unable to find a permanent home for her menagerie of buildings. BLM (Bureau of Land Management), which oversees federal land along the Dalton Highway, had been less than cooperative. "BLM won't give me a lease because . . . I don't have the look they want. They say they want development on the road and they want to support locals. But they came up, took one look at my place, and said they would never, ever lease land to me." So, the Hot Spot goes year to year on a little bit of private-owned land. "I never know whether I will be here next year," Theresa said with both resignation and hope in her voice. "I have to have faith that things will work out the way they are supposed to."

▲ ▲ Theresa turned an old incinerating toilet building into a restaurant.
▲ From the beginning truckers have been Theresa's biggest supporters.
▶ BLM took one look at the place and said they would never lease land to Theresa.

REINDEER FARM

Palmer

What is the most-frequently asked question at the Reindeer Farm in Palmer? According to Myra Boykin, who has worked there three years, it's "You mean reindeer really do exist?" To help the Eskimos, Congress passed a law in 1937 requiring that any reindeer in the territory of Alaska at the time and all of their descendents must be owned by Natives. The federal law survived statehood and today Alaska is the only state where

▲ Reindeer sometimes get a little rowdy while in search of a handout.
▶ and ▶▶ Reindeer like to mingle with visitors to the Reindeer Farm.

such a law applies. In 1987, Tom Williams took a little detour around the law when he imported nineteen reindeer from Tuktoyaktuk ("Tuk" for short) in Canada's Northwest Territories. In 1990, he imported another 165. When I visited, Tom was maintaining a herd of two hundred animals. Everyone knows that reindeer, which are domesticated caribou brought over to North America from Scandinavia, provide Santa with transportation on his annual rounds. I overheard Myra explain a reindeer's abilities to a young girl visiting from Ohio. "Reindeer really do fly," she said. "Get

your parents to buy one, and we'll put it on a plane and fly it to wherever you live." Jokes aside, reindeer serve a couple of niche markets. First, they provide protein for a small group of meat-eaters who get past the concept of consuming a piece of Rudolph, Donner, and Blitzen. Second, for the Asian market, they provide (or at least their antlers do) a primary ingredient for a number of traditional medicines. Luckily for the reindeer, the annually shed antlers are a renewable resource. When reindeer are not otherwise engaged you can find them at the farm mingling with visitors and sometimes getting a little rowdy while in search of a handout. "Will they hurt the kids?" a concerned mom asked Myra as several large bull reindeer crowded around her three small children. "No, they are only interested in food," Myra reassured her. "Just like men," the woman replied without missing a beat.

ARCTIC CIRCLE HOT SPRINGS

Eight miles off the
Steese Highway

▶ When the hot springs were first
discovered a bucket and a towel
were all local miners needed.

Arctic Circle Hot Springs, located 75 miles south of the Arctic Circle, isn't so much a roadside attraction as it is an end-of-the-road attraction. And that may be the biggest obstacle to its success. 🚗 It didn't take long after prospector William Great found the hot springs bubbling out of a hillside in 1891 for the spot to become popular with local gold miners. Though living far from available women, some of the miners nonetheless were interested in a hot bath once in a while. A bucket and a towel were all they needed. 🚗 In 1902, Frank and Emma Leach homesteaded one hundred sixty acres around the spring. They built the lodge and pool and gave the place respectability. For the next thirty years the hot springs, accessible only by wagon over a rough trail or by airplane,

remained a favorite for locals but a challenge for anyone as far away as Fairbanks. On the day the Steese Highway was opened in the 1930s, more than one hundred cars made the trip. Since then, the resort has struggled to draw visitors the 126 miles northeast from Fairbanks. By the time Fairbanks businessman Robert Miller bought the lodge as a retirement home for himself in 1980, even the locals were staying away. In 1997, after making numerous repairs and improvements but frustrated by unsuccessful attempts to work with outside management, Miller turned the place over to LaVerna, his wife of seven years. Together, he and LaVerna continued to make improvements, adding an exercise room, ice cream parlor, and a small conference room. Locals have returned, and folks from Fairbanks seem to fill the place on holidays and weekends. Still, being near the end of a remote, dead-end highway continues to be a disadvantage. "It's kind of quiet here during the week," a local told me as we shared the pool on a quiet Sunday evening. "I don't think the tourists have found this place yet. I think they are afraid of the road, and that's okay with me."

◀ ▲ and ◀ Frank and Emma Leach homesteaded the spring and built the lodge and pool to give the place some respectability.

SOLOMON

Nome-Council Road

▲ and ▶ The town of Solomon has had more lives than a cat.
▶ ▶ The railroad in Solomon was started in 1903 but never completed.

The 73-mile Nome-Council Road traverses some of the richest historical landscape on the Seward Peninsula. Two highlights of the trip, and great examples of tenacity and folly as well, are the remains of the town of Solomon and the nearby Council and Solomon River Railroad. 🚗 Though never equaling the importance of the Nome gold rush, discovery of gold in the nearby Solomon River Valley in 1898 drew several thousand miners. In little time, a supply base and transportation hub blossomed on a sand spit at the mouth of the Solomon River. 🚗 Locating Solomon on a beach at sea level may have seemed like a good idea, but several destructive storms proved otherwise. Each time rowdy waves took out the town, determined miners rebuilt it. By 1904, Solomon was a thriving town of about 2,000 with a post office, three stores, four hotels, and seven saloons. 🚗 Though the wide gently sloping gravel bed of the Solomon River made a good trail for pack horses and wagons, development in the gold fields was constrained by the difficulty and cost of trans-

porting heavy equipment. In 1903, the Western Alaska Construction Company of Chicago obtained a right-of-way to build the first standard-gauge railroad on the Seward Peninsula, between Solomon and Council. 🚗 Initially, construction of terminal facilities (a half-mile inland) and laying of a few miles of track boosted

Solomon's fortunes, but declining gold production and mismanagement by the railroad eventually took their toll. By 1908, the railroad was bankrupt and Solomon nearly deserted. 🚙 Still the town hung on. 🚙 Over the next forty years, Solomon was destroyed once by fire and once by storm, and was rebuilt each time. Later, the area was resurrected as an Eskimo village only to be nearly wiped out by an epidemic. It was heavily damaged by floods and moved twice, the last time to its present location. Finally, as Nome's economy stabilized and Solomon's declined, residents moved on to Nome and other towns with better prospects. 🚙 Even a cat runs out of lives sooner or later.

KEYSTONE CANYON

Richardson Highway
near Valdez

▶ Water cascades down the canyon walls to form an endless array of waterfalls.

In a land blessed by so many extraordinary vistas, driving the narrow stretch of Richardson Highway along the Lowe River through Keystone Canyon may feel claustrophobic. Yet, an amazing amount of beauty is squeezed into those three miles. Keystone Canyon is the result of some serious stream erosion, which began as glaciers melted at the end of the last ice age. Benches on the upper sides of the canyon mark the various floor levels of the U-shaped, glacier-formed valley. Heavy snow that collects on surrounding mountains melts vigorously in the relatively mild maritime climate close to the coast, and the resulting runoff cascades down the steep V-shaped canyon walls to form an endless array of waterfalls. Bridal Veil Falls, towering 500-feet high over the highway and the 100-foot Horsetail Falls are the best known, but dozens of smaller unnamed cascades decorate

the canyon walls too, especially in spring. 🚙 After gold was discovered in the Klondike in 1896, an all-American, all-weather route into the Interior became the Holy Grail of Alaska exploration. In 1898, a U.S. Army expedition under the command of Captain W. R. Abercrombie surveyed a route north through Keystone Canyon that has remained essentially unchanged for the past century. 🚙 The original route was little more than a trail, more suited to winter travel by dog sled than summer travel by wagon. Over the years, improvements were made, but calling this military route a "road" was a bit of a stretch. The first auto to travel from Valdez to Fairbanks (a distance of about 370 miles) through Keystone Canyon completed the trip in a blistering thirteen days in 1913. The "road" along the base of the canyon suffered so many wash outs that it was closed more often than it was open. 🚙 The road was relocated above the canyon floor for a while using a route along the glacial benches christened the Goat Trail. But as the name might suggest, it never made a reasonable alternative to the original route and the road was returned to the bottom of the canyon after World War II. 🚙 Though necessity rather than choice may have decided the route through Keystone Canyon, it remains one of the most beautiful stretches of road in Alaska.

◄ and ▲ The 3-mile stretch of road through Keystone Canyon is one of the most beautiful in Alaska.

CHANDLER'S CASTLE

East End Road

Homer

▶ Steve and Brad made a castle using 3 inches of spray insulating foam.

Back in the early 1980s, Steve Chandler was a full-time foam insulation installer and part-time cannabis grower in Homer. One day, Steve got the idea to spray the outside—not the inside, mind you, the outside—of his small barn-shaped house with three inches of yellow insulating foam. Said friend Brad Hughes by way of explanation: "Steve is an intuitively creative mind with a short attention span." 🚗 "It looked horrible," Brad said with a smile in his voice. "The neighbors were going crazy. He wasn't even a good spray

▲ (Clockwise) These days Chandler's Castle is an abandoned piece of Homer's past bordering on being a neighborhood eyesore.

foamer." 🚙 That was when Steve called Brad, a full-time professional artist, to help him out. "I took one look at the place and said Tudor cottage," Brad continued. "I have no idea where the idea came from. I pulled it out of the top of my head. We made some tools that were like giant cheese shavers, carved it here and there, and painted it." 🚙 According to Brad, Steve lived in the "Tudor cottage" four or five years before making some changes. He got some heavy wire mesh, made circles with the wire, stood them several widths high, sprayed the outside with insulating foam and—presto!—towers. Brad was called in once again. 🚙 "Once I saw the towers, I said we have a castle working here," Brad told me. "I designed a bunch of pieces to make it look like a castle. We re-carved it and repainted it to look like stone." Brad paused, as if to savor the memory. "Steve really liked the whole castle thing." No word on whether his neighbors liked the whole castle thing as well. 🚙 Eventually, Steve got himself into a little trouble and had to leave town. These days Chandler's Castle is an abandoned piece of Homer's past, an intuitively creative roadside attraction bordering on neighborhood eyesore.

LAST WORD

Okay, I admit there have been times working on my Alaska books that I wished Alaska was closer to the size of, say . . .Rhode Island. Alaska is "arterially challenged"—that is, it has few roads. But in the interest of making these stories as geographically diverse as possible, I spent a lot of time on the far-flung roads we have. Getting to some of them hasn't always been easy either. In addition to the more than 22,000 miles I have traveled on Alaska's road system, I have traveled a couple of thousand miles on Alaska's Marine Highway System and more than one thousand miles by air. Note that I am careful in my use of the word "highway" to describe Alaska's roads. Officially, Alaska has seventeen highways, though describing a two-lane gravel monster such as the Denali Highway as a "highway" takes chutzpah or at least a keen sense of humor. Like comparing dog years to human years, a mile traveled on an Alaska "highway" equals about seven miles on a

highway anywhere else in America. Don't get me wrong, I'm not complaining. As folks everywhere constantly remind me, I'm a lucky guy. I get the chance to travel around one of the most beautiful places on earth and to meet some of the most interesting people anywhere. No question, there are worse ways to earn a living.

▶ Harry and Ringa along one of Alaska's seventeen "highways."